Child's Catechism In English And Laguna...

John Menaul

Nabu Public Domain Reprints:

You are holding a reproduction of an original work published before 1923 that is in the public domain in the United States of America, and possibly other countries. You may freely copy and distribute this work as no entity (individual or corporate) has a copyright on the body of the work. This book may contain prior copyright references, and library stamps (as most of these works were scanned from library copies). These have been scanned and retained as part of the historical artifact.

This book may have occasional imperfections such as missing or blurred pages, poor pictures, errant marks, etc. that were either part of the original artifact, or were introduced by the scanning process. We believe this work is culturally important, and despite the imperfections, have elected to bring it back into print as part of our continuing commitment to the preservation of printed works worldwide. We appreciate your understanding of the imperfections in the preservation process, and hope you enjoy this valuable book.

THE CONSONANTS

have their common sounds, except *n* and *t* which have additional sounds.

N n has its common sound and a nasal sound, much like the Spanish ñ (enye) but does not necessarily include the *y*.

This sound is represented by the Spanish ñ. The *y* is added when it takes that sound.

T t has its natural sound, a dental and a palatal sound.

The dental sound is made by placing the tip of the tongue firm against the roots of the upper front teeth. articulating the letter as modified by the following vowel.

This sound is represented by *t* Fr. Cl. It has no similar sound in our languages.

The palatal sound is made by placing the tongue firm and flat against the roof of the mouth, allowing it to relax as the accompanying vowel is sounded.

This sound is represented by *t* shaded. It has no similar sound in our languages.

Each word is pronounced as spelled, giving the letters their Continental or natural sounds.

The accent is generally on the penult.

INTRODUCTION.

The object of translating and printing this little Catechism is to give the Laguna Pueblo Indian people and their children a condensed and simple outline of our Christian Religion.

We took it for granted that the simplest work we could find would be best suited to their understanding; and would also, be the easiest rendered into a nearly literal translation of their Language.

The work of translation has extended over about three years. The Catechism being taught in the Sabbath School, a few questions at a time were carefully translated, when we could secure the help of the Interpreter. Then these questions were gone over with the children till we got the sound of the words as nearly as our alphabet would represent them. On this account words meaning the same thing and having the same person and number are some times differently spelled. The object being not uniformity in spelling so much as to follow the Interpreter as closely as possible; besides at first we did not catch the sounds of many words as clearly as towards the last of the work.

The work of printing has been done in odd hours out of Day School, and as we could find opportunity. As we are only learning the art of printing some of the work is not well done, and several typographical errors escaped our unpracticed eye till it was too late. But the Book is not for the Public, at least in its present form, and hence we do not expect to be exposed to Public criticism. We have already commenced to revise the Laguna translation, and find that even as it is, there is very little improvement to be made, except occasionally where the text may be made a little fuller or where the persons or numbers of flexible words need to be corrected.

This little Catechism gives the Laguna people one complete book in their own Language, we trust that it may be instru-

mental in leading many of them from heathen darkness to the Knowledge of the Only Living and True God.
John Menaul.
Laguna, N. M.
April 1st. 1880.

CATECHISM.

Q. 1. who made you?
   Howe kittueach hishome?
A. GOD.
   DIOS.
Q. 2. What else did God make?
   Zē thick koeach Dios?
A. God made all things.
   Dios koeach seiotse tēe kashe shĕ wytu kashe.
Q. 3. Why did God make you and all things?
   Sekoma koeach Dios hishome shĕ seiotse tēe kashe wytu kashe?
A. For his own glory.
   Dios koeach seiotse tēe kashe wytu kashe nowe tawa kashe.
Q. 4. How can you glorify God?

Qua itye nēsho hishome Dios sēotsipatshe?

A. By loving him, and doing what he commands.

Itye imme hṳmako nēsho skohēmako Dios tēka, stchĕ enyechase seio hĕme zē squeanyekweanishe Dios hinome.

Q. 5. Why ought you to glorify God?

Sekoma shetchkeiame hishome nēsinishe kwae kowyanishe Dios?

A. Because he made me, and takes care of me.

Sekoma stchĕ Dios skoeatch hinome, stchĕ pashoñyoko hinome.

Q. 6. Are there more Gods than one?

Aiyet̓a iske noe Dios?

A. There is only one God.

Sah. Iskĕtsa noe Dios.

Q. 7. In how many persons

does this one God exist?
> Hatso haño immetsa ǀua noe Dios?

A. In three persons.
> Chime haño.

Q. 8. What are they?
> Qua keiya?

A. The Father, the Son, and the Holy Ghost.
> Nashtēa, shĕ keiatch, shĕ Ityetseshe Shatshe.

Q. 9. What is God?
> Zē heityetsa Dios?

A. God is a spirit, and has not a body like men.
> Dios immetsa iske katshats, stchĕ satse hate tinye quae hutstse tsinyetshe, ǀotse ūyopetsko.

Q. 10. Where is God?
> Hateka Dios?

A. God is every where.
> Dios imme seio hate putǀaka.

Q. 11. Can you see God?

Itye hishome ñyokutchsho Dios?

A. No, I cannot see God, but he always sees me.

Sah, satse hinome itye Dios ñyokutchskono, tsko sityotse Dios skokchinkwe hinome.

Q. 12. Does God know all things?

Kolonye Dios seiotse?

A. Yes, nothing can be hid from God.

Ha, satse zē itye nueskomakono tĕimmetseshe Dios.

Q. 13. Can God do all things?

Itye Dios nowechako seiotse tawa?

A. Yes, God can do all his holy will.

Ha, Dios itye seiotse nowĕtchako tawa,

CATECHISM.

imme seiotse stuts kowstcheyaañye kutsitch'añye.

Q. 14. Where do you learn how to love and obey God?

Hate itye ñyowtumitsho sinaischo shĕ ñyotoñyesho shĕ otsetokeie Dios?

A. In the Bible alone.

Nowe imme Bible tēka.

Q. 15. Who wrote the Bible?

Howe kutyach Bible?

A. Holy men, who were taught by the Holy Ghost.

Howe yo tawa hutstse imme sēopĕĕnishe Dios kashe Espiritu Santo.

Q. 16. Who were our first parents?

Howe immetsa seia sanashtēashe hinometitch nastēha naia?

A. Adam and Eve.

Imme Adam imme Eve.

Q. 17. Of what were our

first parents made?

Zē heitye koeach Dios stchinye nashtēa Adam naia Eve?

A. God made the body of Adam out of the ground, and formed Eve from the body of Adam.

Dios koeach stchinye nashtēa Adam imme yae hatse, shĕ imme Dios koeach stchinye naia Eve iske yakuchonye imme nashtēa Adam.

Q. 18. What did God give Adam and Eve besides bodies?

Zē heitye thicka stchinye howetsetch Dios Adam Eve?

A. He gave them souls that could never die.

Dios howetsetch Adam Eve nēskonishe sama sañyostoskonishe.

Q. 19 Have you a soul as

well as a body?

Kutcha hishome iske nĕshonishe thick*a* imme sinye?

A. Yes, I have a soul that can never die.

Ha, sashe iske nĕshonishe sama ñyuslossinishe.

Q. 20. How do you know that you have a soul?

Qua sholoñye hishome nĕshonishe?

A. Because I can think about God and the world to come.

Stchĕ itye hinome notsitchlase Dios kashe, stchĕ itye hinome notsitchlase iska hatse tĕka howetsthoñyekonishe.

Q. 21. In what condition did God make Adam and Eve?

Zē heitye koeach Dios Adam Eve tĕka?

A. He made them holy and happy.

Dios koeach Adam Eve tawatseshe shĕ skeie oĕstcheaañye

Q. 22. What is a covenant?

Zĕ imme iske tsĕoshanishe?

A. An agreement between two or more persons.

Imme iske keimatshe koeachaño eskawᴀ tue haño ko mina iska haño.

Q. 23. What covenant did God make with Adam?

Zĕ tsĕoshanishe koeach Dios eskawa Adam?

A. The covenant of works.

Tsĕoshanishe kowyanishe koɬanitch.

Q. 24. What was Adam bound to do by the covenant of works?

Zē howetsetch Adam Dios tēka tua tsēoshanishe kowyanishe kotanitch?

A. To obey God perfectly.

Adam howetsetch Dios tēka stchĕ noyo otsetokeie Dios sĕka seiotse.

Q. 25. What did God promise in the covenant of works?

Zē heitye howetsetch Dios Adam tēka tua tsēoshanishe kowyanishe kotanitch?

A. To reward Adam with life, if he obeyed him.

Dios howetsetsh Adam tēka stchĕ noyo nētsowako Adam tawa nēkonishe, imme Adam kowyanishe kotanitch ēshechanshe.

Q. 26. What did God threaten in the covenant of works?

Zē sotsimme howetsetch Dios sah kaowtsetokeie Adam, sah pashokono tsēoshanishe kowyanishe kotanitch?

A. To punish Adam with death, if he disobeyed.

Dios howetsetch imme otseꞩañye Adam sotsimme nēkonishe shĕ ēschime, sah kaowtseꞩokeie Adam.

Q. 27. Did Adam keep the covenant of works?

Pashokoꞩo Adam ꞩua tsēoshanishe kowyanishe koꞩanitch?

A. No, he sinned against God.

Sah, sotsimme etsetch Dios tēka.

Q. 28. What is sin?

Zĕ heityetsa sotsimmetseshe?

A. Sin is any want of conformity unto, or transgression of, the law of God.

Sotsimme imme satse etsetcho imme satse nēkoño kwa tawa kowyanishe Dios, shĕ etsetchanshe zĕ heitye Dios kowya pame epech ꞩua sotsimme.

Q. 31. What was the sin of our first parents?

Zē mēsho heityetsa sotsimme sanashtēashe seia?

A. Eating the forbidden fruit.

Kaapyowkwea kuatsishe saimmetseshe ĕkatsanshe Dios.

Q. 32. Who tempted them to do this sin?

Howe seiawełutch sanashtēashe seia enetchaskonishe ļua sotsimme?

A. The devil tempted Eve, and she gave the fruit to Adam.

Swaṭuma seiawēłutch Eve, shĕ Eve sowo kuatsishe Adam.

Q. 33. What befell our first parents, when they had sinned?

Zē kwetsetch hinomeitch seia sanashtēashe hamashu seia sanashtēashe sotsimme etsetchaño?

A. Instead of being holy and happy, they became sinful and miserable.

Imme aiye seiotse tawatsaa shĕ seiotse oēstcheanye, howetshoko sotsitseshe shĕ seiotse sotsimme.

Q. 34. Did Adam act for himself alone in the covenant of works?

Etsetch Adam nowe kutsinyea tua tsēoshanishe kowyanye kotanich?

A. No, he represented all his posterity.

Sah. sēosha seio hĕme keiatchtemeshe.

Q. 35. What effect had the sin of Adam on all mankind?

CATECHISM. 17

Zē kwĕtsechana hutstse seio hañо ļua sotsimme Adam?

A. All mankind are born in a state of sin and misery.

Nako ļua sotsimme Adam seio haño keityasa iske tēka sotsimme shĕ sotsimme-tsheshe.

Q. 36 What is that sinful nature which we inherit from Adam, called?

Kwaka ļua sotsimme skeiaapshe Adam?

A. Original sin.

Tseia sotsimme.

Q. 37. What does every sin deserve?

Zē heitye seio sotsimme ñeitsowa-ñyeko?

A. The wrath and curse of God.

Skutsaiyawañye sotsimme ĕkatsan-ye Dios kashe.

Q. 38. Can any one go to heaven with this sinful nature?

Itye howe ṭowya seia sotsimme heya itye ñyoputṭyo wyṭu?

A. No, our hearts must be changed, before we căn be fit for heaven.

Sah, aie ñyetzipatṭĕko tawa wĕñuska, heya ṭĕimme nuṭapa sochosa howo ñyopskonishe wyṭu.

Q. 39. What is a change of heart called?

Kwaka ṭua naname tawa wĕñuska?

A. Regeneration.

Thickana shĕ tsēa.

Q. 40. Who can change a sinner's heart?

Howwe itye ñyeiyakoko wĕñuska sotsitseshe?

A. The Holy Spirit alone.
Nowe Dios Espiritu Santo.

Q. 41. Can any one be saved through the covenant of works?
Itye howe tawatēya ñyoptyo wytu sĕka tawatēya seoshanshe kotanitch?

A. None can be saved through the covenant of works.
Satse howe itye tawa enetchakoño sĕka tawatēya seoshanshe kotanitch.

Q. 42. Why can none be saved through the covenant of works?
Qua satse howe itye tawanatakoño imme heya seoshanshe kotanitch?

A. Because all have broken it, and are condemned by it.
Sekoma stchĕ seio noyo sotsimme tua etsetchana seoshanshe, shĕ tua etsetchana seoshanshe seio haño kutchoatseko.

Q. 43. With whom did God the Father make the covenant of grace?

Howe tēya koeatch Dios sanashtēashe keia seoshanshe kowstcheyaanye?

A. With Christ his eternal Son.

Jesu Christo tēya keiatch tuitsho.

Q. 44. Whom did Christ represent in the covenant of grace?

Howe kowtsinyea etsetch Jesu Cristo keia seoshanshe kowstcheyaanye?

A. His elect people.

Seio stchohēmako kutchashe.

Q. 45. What did Christ undertake in the covenant of grace?

Zē heitye keiowooh Jesu Cristo keia seoshanshe kowstcheyaanye?

A. To keep the whole law for his people, and to suffer the punishment due to their sins.

Ñyeyokeikonishe kahañotemishe seio tawatseshe, stchĕ bowets{hoko kow{oe nyoo otse{añye kahañotemishe sotsimme tēya.

Q. 46. Did the Lord Jesus Christ ever commit the least sin?

Zē sotsimme etsetch hama suchashetshe Jesu Cristo?

A. No, he was holy, harmless, and undefiled.

Sah, satse hama sotsimme etsetcho, satse sēotsekoyo, satse sotsimmetsaow.

Q. 47. How could the Son of God suffer?

Quae itye kow{oe keiatch Dios.

A. Christ, the Son of God,

became man, that he might obey and suffer in our nature.

Cristo, keiatch Dios, hutstsetsatsetch, stchĕ eskawa iske sutchaah itye nowtseʇokeittu sochooh thick nutsooʇoe sochooh.

Q. 48. What is meant by the Atonement?

Zē heityetsa Atonement?

A. Christ's satisfying divine justice, by his suffering and death, in the place of sinners.

Dios sewēstchea koweianye Jesu Cristo eikashe sotsiteshe tĕka, koeach Jesu Cristo sachotsinñyea sonama kowʇowēshe, shĕ ischime.

Q. 49. What did God the Father undertake in the covenant of grace?

Zē heitye howetsetch Dios Nashtēa keia seoshanshe kowstcheyaanye.

A. To justify and sanctify those for whom Christ should die.

Dios howetsetch keimatshe s‚otsetseshe stchĕ kaowyastemeshe seio sotsimmetseshe kaowyestche stchĕ haño kashe Jesu Cristo koshṭo.

Q. 50. What is justification?

Zē heityetsa keimatshe?

A. It is God's forgiving sinners, and treating them as if they had never sinned.

Imme ṭua Dios seiawaṭeiponeie haño sotsimmetsetchanshe, shĕ ṭua haño hamasho tseosha qua sah sotsimmenaḷakonishe.

Q. 51. What is sanctification?

Zē heityetsa seoyaschimmeshe?

A. It is God's making sinners holy in heart and conduct.

Imme iske koweianye Dios heitye Dios

koeach maēma sityotse tawa někonishe shě veñuska ʇua haño hama sotsimmetsetchana.

Q. 52. For whom did Christ obey and suffer?

Howe haño kaowtsinyea kowtseʇokeie shě kowʇoe eschime Jesu Cristo?

A. For those whom the Father had given him.

Seio ʇua haño howo Nashʇēa Dios etseochanɑ̄tshe.

Q. 53. What kind of life did Christ live on earth?

Zē někonishe kaaiko Jesu Cristo tĕkeispeyesho?

A. A life of poverty and suffering.

Iske někonishe amome shě kowʇoe.

Q. 54. What kind of death did Christ die.

Zē yà koshʇo Jesu Cristo?

A. The painful and shameful death of the cross.

Zē ya sewasa shĕ kañonaañyeko shoketchatse tēya koshṭo.

Q. 55 Who will be saved?

Howe tawa seiateṭa tawakoso?

A. Only those who repent of sin, believe in Christ, and lead holy lives.

Nowe wĕ haño keiyeiṭamishe sotsimme etsetchanshe, shĕ sēohēmatshe Jesu Cristo, shĕ nuṭĕĕkosa shame tawa.

Q. 56. What is it to repent?

Zē heityetsa skeiyeiṭamo?

A. To be sorry for sin, and to hate and forsake it, because it is displeasing to God.

Heya oṭume sotsimmetseshe, shĕ satse sĕkatsaow sotsimmetseshe, shĕ sotsimmetseshe ṭonetchase stchĕ satse Dios ñyokutchtkoño satse ñewĕstcheyasseomaño.

Q. What is it to believe or have faith in Christ?

zē heityetsa stchohēmako kokeimatskoño Jesu Cristo?

A. To trust in Christ alone for salvation.

Naskonishe nowe Jesu Cristo stchĕ tawatseshetsa.

Q. 58. Can you repent and believe in Chtist, by your own power?

Itye hishome neiyeittowsho shĕ kotchēmako hishome Jesu Cristo noyo kutchashe tawatsa?

A. No, I can do nothing good without the help of God's Holy Spirit.

Sah, satse hinome itye tawatse enetchaskoño heitye tawatseshe sah skomasañye-

CATECHISM. 27

tow Dios kashe Espiritu Santo.

Q. 59. How can you get the help of the holy Spirit?

Quae itye tawa ñyeyeinasho ñyomatsañyekutchoma tawaseshe Dios kashe Espiritu Santo?

A. God has told us that we must pray for the Holy Spirit.

Dios squape hinometitch zĕ hinometitch toskowachoma saskama tawatseshe Dios kashe Espiritu Santo.

Q. 60. How long ago is it since Christ died?

Hatso kusheit kaaich Cristo koshttĕshe?

A. More than eighteen hundred years.

Mĕsh meiko kaeich kuts kuts ow a kuts kokomish ow a kuts ow a kuts kusheit kaeitch.

Q. 61. How were pious persons saved before the coming

of Christ?

Quae itye ñupcheiawakosa tawatseshe keimatchshe stotshe tua sĕĕmeshe sañaah howĕtsots Jesu Cristo?

A. By believing in a Saviour to come.

Zē keimats tēa zē ohēmats tēa iske howĕtsthonyekonishe tawañyeacha skwachomanishe Jesu Cristo.

Q. 62. How did they show their faith?

Heitye tsēya ñyeimatsko tua keimatshe stotshe kashe stchohēmako?

A. By offering sacrifices on God's altar.

Sēokamishe sacrifices altar Dios kashe.

Q. 63. What did these sacrifices represent?

Zē heitye kokchana yanye tua sacrifices?

A. Christ, the Lamb of God,

who was to die for sinners.

Jesu Cristo, Ottumish Dios, howe howetsthonyeko ñyusǀoko sotsimmetseshe tēya.

Q. 64. What offices has Christ?

Hatso kaiyokei ka Cristo?

A. Christ has three offices.

Jesu Cristo chimmeĕ ka kaiyokei.

Q. 65. What are they?

Zē heityetsa?

A. The offices of a Prophet, of a Priest, and of a King.

Immetsa kaiyokei Prophet, Priest, King.

Q. 66. How is Christ a prophet?

Quae koǀanitch Jesu Cristo kaiyokei prophet?

A. Because he teaches us the will of God.

Skeisomesh!a seio hĕme koweianishe Dios.

Q. 67. How is Christ a priest?

Quae ko!anitch Jesu Ctisto kaiyokei prest?

A. Because he died for our sins and pleads with God for us.

Stchŭ howskeiyowoh hinometitch sotsstcheyañyeshow, shĕ que!aañyequea Dios tĕka satsotsēñyeya hinometitch.

Q. 68. How is Christ a king?

Quae ko!anitch Jesu Cristo kaiyokei king?

A. Because he rules over us and defends us.

Pashoskwashuma hinometitch shĕ ñyeyowweimēskowashoma hinometitch.

Q. 69. Why do you need Christ as a prophet?

Sekoma katsipatte Jesu Cristo qua prophet?

CATECHISM. 31

A. Because I am ignorant.

Ako sekoma hinome kē satse kwa skoñyemo.

Q. 70. Why do you need Christ for a priest?

Sekoma katsipatte Jesu Cristo qua priest?

A. Because I am guilty.

Ako sekoma hinome imme skotseko.

Q. 71. Why do you need Christ as a king?

Sekoma katsipatte Jesu Cristo qua king?

A. Because I am weak and helpless.

Ako sekoma satse zē ityeetsaow hinome stchĕ satse zē nowweimeskoño.

Q. 72. How many commandments did God give on Mount Sinai?

Hatso koweia Dios howwo tinyeae Kotye Sinai?

A. Ten commandments.

Howetsetch kuts koweia.

Q. 73. What are the ten commandments sometimes called?

Zē iska ĕka ṭua kuts soweianye?

A. The Decalogue.

Decalogue.

Q. 74. What do the first four commandments teach?

Zē howwo eskawachañye hinometitch seia tana koweia?

A. Our duty to God.

Zē hinometitch enetchanasochosa Dios tēka.

Q. 75. What do the last six commandments teach?

Zē howwo eskawachañye iska schis koweia?

A. Our duty to our fellow-men.

Zē hinometitch enetchanasochosa iska haño tĕka.

Q. 76. What is the sum of the ten commandments?

Zē qua natsako seio iske kaeichañye kuts koweia?

A. To love God with all my heart, and my neighbour as myself.

Notse╷okeise Dios seio sewĕñuska seio s╷ka, stchĕ howĕko haño quae hĕmako hinomemĕ.

Q. 77. Who is your neighbour?

Howe howĕko kut╷aah?

A. All my fellow-men are my neighbours.

Seio haño keispeyesho stchaow.

Q. 78. Is God pleased with those who love and obey him?

Sewĕstcheya Dios ʇua haño sēotseʇokeitshe Dios shĕ etsetchanatshe quae Dios koweianishe?

A. Yes, he says, "I love them that love me."

Ha, Dios ĕkatsa, "Hinome skotseʇokeitshe ʇua haño wĕĕ haño skotseʇokeitshe."

Q. 79. Is God displeased with those who do not love and obey him?

Immeʇa sah satsesewĕstcheaow Dios ʇua haño tĕka sah kaowtseʇokeitshe Dios tĕka, shĕ satse etsetchanatʇow Dios tĕka?

A. "Yes, God is angry with the wicked every day."

Ha, "Dios kotsaiowa sityotse sashkama ʇua haño sotskeitañye tĕka."

CATECHISM. 35

Q. 80. What is the first commandment?

Heitye imme tseia tseoweianye?

A. The first commandment is, Thou shalt have no other gods before me.

Tseoweianye immetsa ckatsa Dios, Satse naname Dios nashoño eisopsho eie ityee stchesho hinome.

Q. 81. What does the first commandment teach us?

Zē heitye squape lua tseia tseoweianye?

A. To worship God alone.

Dios nowe etsetch.

Q. 82. What is the second commandment?

Heitye imme hamasho tseoweianye?

A. The second commandment is, Thou shalt not make

unto thee any graven image, or any likeness of any thing that is in heaven above, or that is in the earth beneath, or that is in the water under the earth. Thou shalt not bow down thyself to them nor serve them; for I the Lord thy God am a jealous God, visiting the iniquity of the fathers upon the children, unto the third and fourth generation of them that hate me; and showing mercy unto thousands of them that love me and keep my commandments.

Hamasho tseoweianye immetsa ikatsa Dios. Satse enetchashoño hishome noyo

CATECHISM. 37

seio saimmetseshe, shĕ satse iska zē seio sityachanishe zē saimmetseshe imme zē weitu kashe, shĕ satse zē imme ʇua hatse tĕka, shĕ satse zē imme tsēañeko thicka sits tĕka nutseaa hatse tĕka; satse hishome nowēteyashoño ʇua saimmetseshe sityachanishe tĕka stchĕ satse hishome ʇua saimmetseshe sityachanishe tĕka enetchashoño; stchĕ ʇkatsa Dios, hinome imme kutcha Dios hishome, immetsa hinome iske Dios zē sĕka ñyocheimeskoma, hinome neitsowase sotsimmetseshe nashtĕa naia kashe keiatchtemeshe tĕka chimmeatanowa yoko ʇua haño sakaowtse okeitshe hinome tĕka; shĕ hinome iske Dios etsetch tawa anye nowya kuts kuts ow a kuts yoko ʇua haño skotse okeitshe hinome tĕka shĕ pashokosasthe sowweianye.

Q. 83. What does the second commandment teach us?

Zē squape ʇua hamasho tsēoweianye?

A. To worship God in a proper manner, and to avoid idolatry.

ļua tseoweianye howetsetch, Dios nowe etsetch kwa heitye koweia Dios, shĕ yokota seio saimmetseshe sityachanishe.

Q. 84. What is the third commandment?

Heitye imme chimmeŭ tseoweianye?

A. The third commandment is, Thou shalt not take the name of the Lord thy God in vain; for the Lord will not hold him guiltless that taketh his name in vain.

Chimmeŭ tseoweianye imme, ĕkatsa Dios, Satse hishome ĕnatsashoño saimmetseshe ċkashe Dios kutchashe; stchĕ Dios satse ñyo,oñekoño ļua haño tĕka sashamequeļoñyeme satse sĕotseko ļua hutstse koh tĕka saimmetseshe ċkashe Dios tĕka.

Q. 85. What does the third commandment teach us?

Zĕ howoh eskawaechañye ṭua chimmeĕ?

A. To reverence God's name, word, and works.

ṭua tsēoweianye howoh eskawaechañye hinometitch imme tawa ñutchamashe imme ĕkashe, shĕ ĕkatsanshe, shĕ koweianishe Dios kashe.

Q. 86. What is the fourth commandment.

Heitye imme ṭana tsēoweianye?

A. The fourth commandment is, Remember the Sabbath day to keep it holy. Six days shalt thou labour and do all thy work; but the seventh day is the Sabbath of the Lord thy God: in it thou shalt not do any work, thou, nor thy son, nor thy daughter, nor thy man-servant, nor thy maid-servant, nor thy cattle, nor thy stranger that is within thy gates: for in six days the Lord made heaven and earth, the sea, and all that in them is, and rested the seventh day: wherefore the Lord blessed the Sabbath day, and hallowed it.

tana tsĕowaianye imme, ĕkatsa Dios; ĕĕonye imme sastche nowanachashonishe domĕko weitsastche pashoñyosho tawatseshe. Schis seie ñoļanitchsho shĕ enyetchasho seio kutch'añyechañye; imme stchĕ meityin seie imme immenaļako owanachane kutchanatshe Dios tĕka: satse weie domĕko nowĕchashoño zē oļañyechane, hishome, thick kutchamuțe, thick kutchamak, thick butstse kutchoļawĕshe, thick koh kutchoṭawĕshe, thick kutchṭashe, thick howo kutchowatsinishe eie kaapshe keia tseama kutchasho: stchɜ̆ schis seie Nashtēa Dios koeach hatse howaka, seits, seiotse tēa ĕkashe, shĕ meityin kḁwanatcha Dios: stchĕ ṭua etsetch seṭu Dios seie nowanachashonishe dom ko, shɜ̆ ṭua koeach tawatseshe.

Q. 87. What does the fourth commandment teach us?

Zē howoh eskawachane hinometitch ṭua ṭana tseoweianye?

A. To keep the Sabbath holy.

Pashoñyoskonishe nowanachaskonishe domēko kwa koweianishe Dios.

Q. 88. What day of the week is the Christian Sabbath?

Heitye imme sastche Nowanachako Christiano?

A. The first day of the week, called the Lord's day.

Imme seia sastche, heitye imme ĕka domēko imme ĕnatsako sastche Jesu Cristo.

Q. 89. Why is it called the Lord's day?

Sekoma ĕka domĕko sastche Jesu Cristo kashe?

A. Because on that day Christ rose from the dead.

Stchĕ ḷua weie sastche Jesu Cristo tsɜ̄ tsēa shomo tĕka shĕ yokosthok.

Q. 90. How should the Sabbath be spent?

Shĕ zɜ̄ enyetchanasochosa imme yo ĕ sastche domĕkotsĕ?

A. In prayer and praise, in hearing and reading God's word, and in doing good to our fellow-men.

Imme amoma atsaanye, shɜ̄ owēstcheanye Dios tĕka, shɜ̄ ñyekaskonishe shɜ̄ ñyokchankweaskonishe Dios kashe ɩkatsanshe, shĕ tawanaˌaskonishe hañoˌ tĕka.

Q. 91. What is the fifth commandment?

Heitye imme tama tsēoweianye?

A. The fifth commandment is, Honor thy father and thy mother, that thy days may be long upon the land which the Lord thy God giveth thee.

Tama tsēoweianye imme, ĕkatsa Dios Potseḻokeie kutchanashtēa kutchanaia, heya nēshonishe nitchkonishe ḻua hatse tēka howo ĕ kuḻuchanētshe kutchanashtēa Dios.

Q. 92. What does the fifth commandment teach us?

Zē squape hinometitch ḻua tama tsēoweianye?

A. To love and obey our parents and teachers.

Ohēmaṭye otseḻokeie hinometitch sanashtēashe sanaiashe shĕ skeisomĕshṭanishe.

Q. 93. What is the sixth commandment?

Heitye imme schis tsēoweianye?

A. The sixth commandment is, Thou shalt not kill.

Schis tsēoweianye imme, ĕkatsa Dios, Satse nowṭashoño.

Q. 94. What does the sixth commandment teach us?

Zē squape hinometitch ṭua schis tsēoweianye?

A. To avoid angry passions.

Stchĕ shatchkaiameshe pashoñyoskonishe sotsimme.

Q. 96. What is the seventh commandment?

Heitye imme mytyin tsēoweianye?

A. The seventh command- ment is, Thou shalt not commit adultery.

Mytyin tsēoweinye imme, ĕkatsa Dios, Satse sotsimme enyetchashoño, satse howwe ñyĕnitchtēaskoño sa imme hutstse kuchashe sa imme koh kutchashe.

Q. 96. What does the seventh commandment teach us?

Zē squape hinometitch ʇua mytyin tsēoweianye?

A. To be pure in heart, language, and conduct.

Imme enetchasho tawa notsitchʇasho showwēnuska shĕ tawa enatsasho, shĕ shame ñyĕnitchtēasho.

Q. 97. What is the eighth commandment?

Heitye imme kokomish tsēoweianye?

A. The eighth commandment is, Thou shalt not steal.

Kokomish tsēoweianye imme, ĕkatsa Dios Satse saimme kutchashe ñiyowoshoño.

Q. 98. What does the eighth commandment teach us?

Zē squape hinometitch ḷua kokomish tsēoweianye?

A. To be honest and industrious.

Pashoonye tawa čsashe hishome, shĕ noḷanitchsho.

Q. 99. What is the ninth commandment?

Heitye imme mioka tsēoweianye?

A. The ninth commandment is, Thou shalt not bear false witness against thy neighbour.

Meioka tsēoweianye imme, ĕkatsa Dios, Satse ĕnatsashoño haño tĕka sa keimatshe sa sḷutshe.

Q. 100. What does the ninth commandment teach us?

Zē squape hinometitch ḷua meioka tsēoweianye?

A. To tell the truth.
Zē keimatse zē stots eatsanye.

Q. 101. What is the tenth commandment?
Heitye imme kuts tsēoweianye?

A. The tenth commandment is, Thou shalt not covet thy neighbour's house, thou shalt not covet thy neighbour's wife, nor his man-servant, nor his maid-servant, nor his ox, nor his ass, nor any thing that is thy neighbour's.
Kuts tsēoweianye imme, ĕkatsa Dios, Satse ñyotyĕtawatsshoño kama eiskawa kutchaamishe, satse ñyotyĕtawatsshoño kowkwe eiskawa kutchaamishe, ko paɬo sēoɬawēshe tyēka, ko paɬo weyes katyashe, ko paɬo horo katyashe, ko paɬo zē kashe eiskawa kutchaamishe.

Q. 102. What does the tenth commandment teach?

Zē squape ṭua kuts tsēoweianye?

A. To be content with our lot.

Ñyewowstcheya squachomanishe.

Q. 103. Can any man keep these ten commandments perfectly?

Itye howe hutstse koh pashoñyoko sĕka maēma enetchako ṭua kuts tsēoweianye?

A. No mere man since the fall of Adam, ever did or can keep the ten commandments perfectly.

Satse haṭye nowe hutstse koh, imme yo ĕ Adam sotsimmeetsetch, mēsho itye, ko satse itye pasho sĕka maēma enetchako ua kuts tsēoweianye.

Q. 104. Of what use is the ten commandments?

Zē heitye tawatsaska hinometitch ȶēka ȶua kuts tsēoweianye?

A. They teach us our duty, and show us our need of a Saviour.

ȶua kuts tsēoweianye squape tawatsa. shĕ anyĕtseshe enyechashonishe, ko thick ñyuwatsipsquachoma iske sēeipatyeshe sēeinowēshe Jesu Cristo.

Q. 105. What is prayer?

Zē heitye amomaotchanye?

A. Prayer is asking God, for things which He has promised to give.

Amomaotchanye imme nēpĕȶako Dios ȶua tawa zē heitye howwo eskawachanetshe hinometitch.

Q. 106. In whose name

should we pray?

Howe kowtsinyea itye amomaatsanye Dios tēka?

A. Only in the name of Christ.

Nowe Jesu Cristo kowtsinyea kashe tēya.

Q. 107. What has Christ given us to teach us how to pray?

zē howoskawaechañye Jesu Cristo hinometitch qua itye amoma nuchatsea sochosa hinometitch?

A. The Lord's prayer.

ʇua amomatsanye Jesu Cristo kashe, qua ʇuitsho immenaʇakonishe sanashtēashe.

Q. 108. Repeat the Lord's prayer.

Oēshaʇyeʇanye amomatsanye Jesu Cristo kashe.

CATECHISM. 51

OUR FATHER which art in heaven, hallowed be thy name. Thy kingdom come. Thy will be done in earth, as it is in heaven. Give us this day our daily bread; And forgive us our debts, as we forgive our debtors; And lead us not into temptation, but deliver us from evil. For thine is the kingdom, and the power, and the glory, for ever. Amen.

Sanashtĕashe hishome wytu kutchameshe Tawaepech eshashe tēya, ṭoĕ hatse kutchashe. Epech kutchowstcheyañye, imme tĕe hatse tĕka qua weitu ĕetseshe imme hĕmako. Qua skwaatsipatshe howwo ekawachañye weie sastche saskama. Shĕ quawaṭeiponeie sotsimme esechanatshe hinometitch ṭaah qua hishometitch skwawaṭeiponeinishe imme hĕmako kwawaṭeiponeie, Pashme kwawahĕĕtsanye ñyowteitskonishe, mame pashoñuwatchoma tuwachoma satawatseshe: Stchĕ nowe kutcha hishome hatse, ityekuṭa, tawatseshe tuitsho ñuṭakonishe. Amen.

Q. 109. How many petitions are there in the Lord's Prayer?

Hatso ñyepĕṭawa sochosa ṭua amomatsanye Jesu Cristo kashe?

A. There are six.

Schis ñyepĕṭawa sochosa.

Q. 110. What is the first petition?

Heitye imme tseia ñyepĕ‡awa sochosa?

A. "Hallowed be thy name."

"Tawa epech eshashe tēya."

Q. 111. What do we pray for in the first petition?

Zē heitye noow‡ana sochosa ‡ua tseia ñyepĕ‡awa sochosa?

A. That God's name may be honoured by us and all men.

Stchĕ hinome shĕ seio haño neokeisochosa nowtse‡okeisochosa kashe Dios.

Q. 112. What is the second petition?

Heitye imme hamasho ñyepĕ‡wa sochosa?

A. "Thy kingdom come."

"‡oĕ hatse kutchashe."

Q. 113. What do we pray for in the second petition?

Zē heitye noowḷana sochosa ṭua tue ñyepĕḷawa sochosa?

A. That the gospel may be preached in all the world, and believed and obeyed by us all and all men.

Soowḷana ṭua ĕkatsanshe Bible Dios kashe imme ĕkatsanshe seio keispeyesho, shē hinometitch thick seio haño squahēmako, sowtseḷokeiṭyow ṭua ĕkatsanshe Dios kashe.

Q. 114. What is the third petition?

Heitye imme chimeŏ ñyepĕḷawa sochosa?

A. "Thy will be done in earth, as it is in heaven."

"Epech kutchowstcheyañye immeŏ tēe hatse tēka qua weiṭyu ĕetseshe imme hĕmako."

Q. 115. What do we pray for in the third petition?

Zē heitye noowṭana sochosa ṭua chimeŏ ñyepĕṭawa sochosa?

A. That men on the earth may serve God, as the angels do in heaven.

Stchŏ seio haño ṭua hatse tĕka chuwahēmachotseṭokeie chowaṭañyecha sityotse saskama Dios tĕka, ṭaah imme etsetchana angels weiṭyu.

Q. 116. What is the fourth petition.

Heitye imme tana ñyepĕṭawa sochosa?

A. "Give us this day our daily bread."

"Kwa squatsipatshe howo ĕkawachañye weie sastche."

Q. 117. What do we pray for in the fourth petition?

Zĕ heitye ñyepĕṯawa sochosa ṯua tana noowṯana sochosa?

A. That God would give us all things needful for our bodies and souls.

Noowṯana sochosa zē nowya naskonishe thick tawa nēskonishe ñunatsaskonishe.

Q. 118. What is the fifth petition?

Heitye imme tama ñyepĕṯawa sochosa?

A. "And forgive us our debts, as we forgive our debtors."

"Shĕ quawaṯeiponeie sotsimme esechanatshe hinometitch, ṯaah qua hishometitch shwawaṯeiponeimishe imme hĕmako kwawaṯeiponeie."

Q. 119. What do we pray for in the fifth petition?

CATECHISM. 57

Zē heitye ñyepĕtawa sochasa ʇua tama noowʇana sochosa?

A. That God would pardon our sins for Christ's sake, and enable us to forgive those who have injured us.

Zē Dios ñyohēmashomanishe maēma ñyoskonishe Jesu Cristo quawaʇeiponeie squawaʇeiponeie sastchaimmetchanishe, shĕ howe kwawachañye hinometitch tawa owēstcheaanye quwawaʇeiponeie iska howe haño howe sotsimme kositchʇanshe etsetchanshe hinome tĕka.

Q. 120 What is the sixth petition?

Heitye imme schis ñyepĕtăwa sochosa?

A. "And lead us not into temptation, but deliver us from evil."

"Satse ñyewahĕĕtsañye ʇyuwatchomaño mame pasho ñyuwatchoma tyuwatchoma sotsitseshe."

Q. 121. What do we pray for in the sixth petition?

Zē heitye ñyepĕtawa sochosa tua schis noowŧtana sochosa?

A. That God would keep us from sin.

Stchĕ Dios pashosquatchoma itye seio tawatseshe sastchaimmechanshe.

Q. 122. How many sacraments are there?

Hatsotsape sacraments?

A. There are two.

Immetsapa tue.

Q. 123. What are they?

Zē heityetsa?

A. Baptism and the Lord's Supper.

Baptism thick Cena Jesu Cristo kashe.

CATECHISM. 59

Q. 124. Who appointed these sacraments?

Howe howwo eskawachañye skeiowoh?

A. The Lord Jesus Christ.

Señor Jesu Cristo.

Q. 125 Why did Christ appoint these sacraments?

Sekoma howe eskawachañye Cristo ļua sacraments?

A. To distinguish his disciples from the world, and to comfort and strengthen them.

Imme heya ļyemenuļapa sochosa ñyowahēmaskwatchoma kahañoļyemishe, shĕ heya ñyowowstcheaskwatchoma kahañoļyemishe, shĕ mame tawa kahañoļyemishe.

Q. 126. What sign is used in baptism?

Zē heitye kweļyumetchañye etsetch

ǂua Baptism?

A. The washing with water.

Anaweistcheme sits ǂyeah.

Q. 127. What does this signify?

Zē heitye kwanatsako ǂua?

A. That we are cleansed from sin by the blood of Christ.

Stchĕ matse kashe Jesu Cristo hinometitch imme heya nowakeia sotchosa seio satawatseshe sotsitseshe.

Q. 128. In whose name are we baptized?

Howe ĕkashe sochashe imme baptized?

A. In the name of the Father, and of the Son, and of the Holy Ghost.

Ekashe Sanashtēa Dios, Nashtēa,

Keiatch, Espirtu Santo.

Q. 129. Who are to be baptized?

Howe haño immenaḷako baptized?

A. Believers and their children.

Tua haño sēwahēmatshe shĕ keiatch-ṭyemishe:

Q. 130. Why should infants be baptized?

Sekoma wak sits nētchaseoma?

A. Because they have a sinful nature and need a Saviour.

Stchĕ ḷona sotsimme notsitchḷako, shĕ ñyetsipatṭyeko iske kosomishe.

Q. 131. Does Christ care for little children?

Pashoñyotyo Jesu Cristo thick wak?

A. Yes, for he says, Suffer

the little children to come unto me, and forbid them not, for of such is the kingdom of Heaven.

Haah, Jesu Cristo ĕkatsa, Pame wak shĕ pame ponamatsa wak howetsthope sēpsho hinome, stchĕ wakatsa imme hatse kah weityu.

Q. 132. To what does your baptism bind you?

Zē heitye sĕka enyechashonishe kutcha howe esecha ḷua sits ñyetcha kochomanishe?

A. To be a true follower of Christ.

Heya saskama sityotse tawañuḷashonishe Jesu Cristo kashe.

Q. 133. What is the Lord's Supper?

Zĕ ḥeityetsa Cena Jesu Cristo kashe?

A. The eating of bread and drinking of wine, in remembrance of the sufferings and death of Christ.

Imme kope pah shĕ thick kuska vino, imme ñyotyumekonishe ĕĕñyokonishe saimmetseshe satawatseshe shĕ koshto Jesu Cristo kashe.

Q. 134. What does the bread represent?

Zē heitye howwo eskawachañye hinometitch tua pah?

A. The body of Christ broken for our sins.

Howwo tsinye Jesu Cristo kashe ĕskawachañye heya sotsimme etsetchanatshe ñyĕwakeiaskwachomanishe hinometitch.

Q. 135. What does the wine represent?

Zē heitye squape ṭua vino?

A. The blood of Christ shed for our salvation.

Imme matse Jesu Cristo kashe sewatsemonishe heya tawañuṭapa sochosa hinometitch.

Q. 136. Who should partake of the Lord's Supper?

Howe itye ñyopĕko ṭua Cena Jesu Cristo kashe?

A. Only those who repent of their sins, believe in Christ for salvation, and love their fellow-men.

Wĕĕ hañó nowe howwe keieityemishe sotsimmetseshe, shĕ ṭua haño sēohēmatshe kashe Jesu Cristo nowe seio tawa kashe tawa nēskonishe, shĕ ṭua haño sēohēmatshe ṭua tawa ĕkatsanshe Jesu Cristo kashe nakonishe haño.

Q. 137. Did Christ remain in the tomb after his crucifixion?

Shĕ eiĕtya ļona Jesu Cristo kosṭyesho?

A. No, he rose from the tomb on the third day after his death.

Sah, Jesu Cristo sē tsēa thickina chime sastche hamasho kashe koshṭyo.

Q. 138. Where is Christ now?

Haṭye imme Jesu Cristo weie ka?

A. In heaven, interceding for sinners.

Jesu Cristo immetsa weiṭyu ka koḷanitcha sachutsinēya sotsimme esetchanatshe ṭyēya.

Q. 139. Will he come again?

Howetsoñyeṭyo thickina Jesu Cristo?

A. Yes, at the last day, Christ will come to judge the world.

Ha, imme yo ĕ seio sastche, Jesu Cristo howwetsonyeko stchĕ sēotseko ñyetchako seio haño.

Q. 140. What becomes of men at death?

Shĕ zē heitye howwetsoñyko haño tyēka koshto?

A. The body returns to dust, and the soul goes into the world of spirits.

Tsinye hatse yae tyēka ñyopko, shĕ weñuska soñyeko ñyetseko ñyenitchtēako wenuska tyēka.

Q. 141. Will the bodies of the dead be raised to life again?

Shĕ thickina sē ñyēatyo tsinye haño koshto?

A. Yes, "the trumpit shall sound and the dead shall be raised."

Ha, "Imme noweiako Dios shĕ koshto sē ñyeako howetstoñyeko shomo tyēka.

Q. 142. What will become of the wicked in the day of judgment?

Shē heitye zē nako sotsimme hañostcheshe imme yoĕ sastche Dios sēotseko ñyeatchaskwachoma?

A. They will be cast into hell.

Sotsimme hañotseshe sotsimme nako sotsimme tyēka ĕ thoñyeko.

Q. 143. What is hell?

Zē heityetsa sotsimmetseshe shomo?

A. A place of dreadful and

endless torment.

Imme iske mame skeie sotsimme shĕ tyuitsho otsełanye sotsimmenałako.

Q. 144. What will become of the righteous?

Shĕ heitye zē nako tawa sēohēmatshe haño?

A. They will be taken to heaven.

Imme haño sēohēmatshe nako weityu Dios kashe.

Q. 145. What is heaven?

Zē heityetsa weityu?

A. A glorious and happy place where the righteous shall be for ever with the Lord.

weityu imme iske zē seiotse tawatseshe seiotse añyĕtseshe seiotse keimatshe imme eie seiotse keimatshe sēohēmatshe

CPSIA information can be obtained at www.ICGtesting.com
Printed in the USA
LVOW03s2303160914

404336LV00022B/788/P